The
Conversation
Of
Merachefet

Indulca mei radices.

A Book of Secrets

by

C. JoyBell C.

Photo on front cover of book by Kari Strand, an aspiring professional photographer and a stay-at-home mom of two young boys. When she is not busy chasing her boys around; she is either taking pictures with her camera, knitting, crocheting or quilting. A sample of her photography can be found at: http://jpgmag.com/people/kariberi

All books by C. JoyBell C. are printed in
the U.S.A., Great Britain and Continental Europe.

ISBN: 1484120000
ISBN- 978-1484120002

www.cjoybellc.com
authorcjoybellc@gmail.com

To you who seeks,
believes and asks.

To you with eyes
full of wonder.

Introduction

The Hebrew word *merachefet* is the 18'th word in the Jewish Torah, and is the essence of *Chet*, which is the 8'th letter in the Hebrew alphabet (the *Alef–Beit*).

The Hebrew letter Chet is formed from the Hebrew letters *Vav* and *Zayin* which represent "light descending from God" and "light ascending to God," respectively. In this certain give-and-take relationship with the two directions of the travel of light, we are already introduced to a moving "pattern" similar to a "dance." There is a "give and take", a "descend and ascend," a "reveal and conceal." This dance of coexisting patterns displayed through these variants of perspective, in itself gives form to the letter Chet which has always been believed by Sages and Rabbis to embody the life force of life itself. Chet, in itself, personifies the gateway to infinity, resurrection of the dead, the life force of life itself, the life force of the soul, the life force of the body, and the essential unity with God.

Again, the essence of the 8'th letter, Chet, is the 18'th word of Torah, merachefet, which means "hovering" in English. Merachefet is the embodiment of the "Divine Relationship," the perfect balance, in between God and His creation. "Touching yet not touching" is the most accurate and simple (although paradoxical) way to describe this Divine Relationship. Just as a parent eagle hovers over her nest while feeding her offspring thus sustaining them while not actually touching them— keeping them alive and nourishing them without landing on them (which would crush them)— so we gain a visual of what merachefet means!

We must be able to see in this essence of "hovering," what is represented therein, which is, the power to enter the mysteries of one's own soul and thereafter return to worldly consciousness! Merachefet is actually the materialization of raw power! The ability to enter into the mysteries of one's own soul and to stand at the gateway to infinity and enter in; but then to still be able to fulfill daily tasks in life— this is the power of power, the materialization of that drop essence of what it means to be powerful! There may be a more root-based power residing in the everyday individual who is able to commune with and within his own soul while walking down the street, talking to friends, going to the grocery store; than there is in those who strive so hard to separate themselves from the world lest they no longer be able to receive of the mysteries of The Kingdom Within.

"Chet" has always been my own personal energy. Even during my childhood, I existed in the "in and out," I dwelt at the gateway of infinity! It was child's play for me to contemplate the mysteries of the soul and the universe, while on the playground or in the classroom or while sitting alone. It is in this light that I have entitled my book *The Conversation of Merachefet.*

Since I was a young girl, I have internally asked myself questions and given myself the answers to those questions (similar to having an inward conversation with myself.) I used to write all the "revelations" into little notebooks of mine and when my father would ask me what I was doing, I would say, "I'm writing down what God is telling me." Of course, my father laughed at me, but now as an adult I still "write down what God is telling me," I share it with the whole world and apparently, many people are thankful for that! What people do not realize is that before all of my "quotes" came to be, there existed my "conversations." I am quoted all over the world for things that I say which people claim have "saved their souls" but has anyone stopped to ask where it all began, how it all starts and where it is all materialized? Let me tell you now that it is all conceived during my moments of merachefet! Moreover, the tagline for this whole book, as you can see, is *Indulca mei radices*, which is Latin for "Sweeten my roots." I gave my book this tagline because I believe that the drop essence of the words within are intended to sweeten a soul at its roots— to inject sweetness at the root-level of the spirit. This Latin phrase is my original creation (to the best of my knowledge) and I can whisper it to myself when I feel that I need to sweeten my roots and remove any negativity that is creeping its way into my life.

When I wrote down this conversation in a moleskin notebook some three years ago, I wrote it under the title *Conversations with Venus*, then later changed it to *Conversations with Aphroselene*. You see, I always wear a moonstone bracelet around my wrist, or when I do not want to wear it around my wrist, I place it in my handbag. I later learned that the ancient Greeks called the moonstone "Aphroselene" as a combination of the goddesses *Aphrodite* and *Selene*. I noticed while looking into the moonstone cabochons around my wrist, that I could see the warm light of the moon reflected in anything! Whether it was day or night— it didn't matter! Everything always glowed with the mild gentleness of the moon, through my moonstones! This caused me to reflect upon the nature of conversing with one's own soul, how the image of my own soul could be reflected back to me no matter the time of day or year, no matter what circumstance I was in! It is by this reason I was inspired to decide upon a working title of *Conversations with Aphroselene*, alluding to the conversations with my own soul! However, after discovering the Alef–Beit, I am convinced that the merachefet of the Hebrew letter Chet, more effectively embodies the meaning of this book. I initially wanted it to appear as *The Conversations of Merachefet* (the word *conversation* being in plural form) but then it dawned on me to present the whole book as a single, streamlined "conversation," hence the current title. That nature holds true to the circumstances by which I wrote my book, in the first place! It was always a continuing conversation that I returned to repeatedly to fulfill. I would write in my notebook, then leave and pick up right where I left off the next time I picked my pen up.

As you can see for yourself, the whole gist of this book is comprised entirely of a single, raw conversation during which there are no third parties and no narrations taking place. The shifting state of mind of the speaker is made evident purely through the fashioning of key words and letters (so please pay attention to that.)

As the conversation begins, I want you to take it into your own setting! If you are in a coffee shop, then imagine the conversation is taking place right beside you and you are eavesdropping in on it! On the other hand, if you are more of the romantic type, then go ahead and imagine the conversation taking place between yourself and the moon during a mellow evening in a rose garden by a stream of bubbling spring water! Alternatively, perhaps the scenario should change as yours changes! Walk with this conversation, incorporate it into an entire day in your life, bring it with you and listen to the voices speaking wherever it may be that you wander! It is all up to you! After all, it would not be "merachefet" without the ability to reveal something unexpected and hidden whilst going about the expected and apparent moments of your life!

While I "hover" in this book, it is my desire that you not only find your answers in my hovering, but that you exercise the ability to hover, as well! Chew on this as you chew on your breakfast, your lunch and your dinner! So let there be life! May there be Chet! *Indulca mei radices.*

Resources:
Information gathered from the author's own studies of the teachings of Rabbi Harav Yitzchak Ginsburgh (Gal Einai Institute). "The Hebrew Letters. Chet: The Life Dynamic of Run and Return." Inner.org. Accessed March 30, 2013.

The Conversation Begins

"*D*o you believe in destiny?"

"How can I not believe in Destiny, when there is no difference between my memories and my dreams at night! There is no difference in their realities! And if I dream something first, I remember it later when I am actually in the place or in front of the person that I dreamt of. Days later. Or years later. Destiny— she walks with me."

"What is destiny then? And what about fate?"

"Destiny is colossal. Colossal and undefeated. The colossal mergence of past, present and future. Before and after, now and later, then and now. She is no respecter of time, no follower of space. She remembers the dreams you have forgotten and dreams for you the memories you left behind. It is all about you. And mountains will bow down and oceans separate, for you!"

"And what about fate?"

"Fate and Destiny are not friends. They do not walk together and Destiny does not acknowledge fate."

"How are the two different?"

"Fate lies to you. Along with fate comes the encounter of fear. Fate tells you: "No matter what you want, this is what will happen to you. Regardless of what you desire, this is what you will have." Meanwhile, fate has no true power over anything. It is her friend named fear who has the power that she boasts of. And fear only has power when you choose to give it to him."

"What do you think of the nature of relationship between fear and chance?"

"I have learned to look at things this way: *if I never get a second chance, how would I wish I did this?* I ask myself that question, and then I do it in that way which I would answer it. In case you do not get a second chance, look at everything as if you only have once chance at it! In case you only get one chance, don't be afraid!"

"So you mean fear could keep you away from your destiny if you give into it?"

"I don't think Destiny can be conquered by fear. But fear can conquer *you*. And if you are going to have only one chance at something in a long while, you don't want to be afraid!"

"And if you are afraid?"

"If you are afraid, then that is a chance to be brave!"

"But what if you are afraid and you don't take the chance to be brave?"

"In that case, you will spend many a lonely night later on... days later, months later, years later... thinking of how you would have done it differently... seeing everything all over again in your mind... wishing you weren't afraid because if you weren't, it could have been something totally different!"

"So you believe in mistakes?"

"What do you mean?"

"So you believe in regretting your choices? In regrets? Mistakes?"

"The only things I consider to be mistakes are the things I did or didn't do, because of fear! Of course, if I were to ever do something to hurt another life, or my own, that would be a mistake in and of itself whether or not I was afraid, but that's a different conversation!"

"What if you weren't afraid... but then lost anyway?"

"If I wasn't afraid, then I never lost! If I was brave, honest and true; I never lost! Never. I would rather risk looking like a fool, than not, if in the process of looking like a fool I am brave, honest and true!"

"So, about destiny, perchance I want to walk with her, what must I do?"

"I don't think that your relationship with Destiny can exist in the light of your thinking there is something you can do in order to have her. Because I cannot imagine her walking with someone who is thinking in such a way. The colossal Destiny— taking your hand because of *your own* efforts? I hardly see that as possible! In fact, I believe that Destiny comes along, grabs ahold of you, hits you hard in the face and shakes you! She shakes you until all that you thought you knew and all that you thought you didn't know, falls away! And you find yourself in the gutter with a bloody nose! Then while you are getting up out of the gutter, you finally know which road to take! And it's the most beautiful thing! You know which road to take, in the shining light of the absence of all the things you thought you were that you really weren't and all the things you thought you weren't but you really were!"

"So destiny... she is not of an elitist upbringing? That's funny, because I always thought her to be of the prim and proper breed!"

"Destiny is real. And she's not mild-mannered. She will come around, hit you in the face and knock you over and before you know what hit you, you are naked! Stripped of everything you thought you knew, everything you thought you didn't know and there you are! A bloody nose, bruises all over you and naked! And it's the most beautiful thing!"

"When does one meet destiny?"

"When one is free and not bound. That's when one meets Destiny; Destiny does not walk with the slave man."

"What is this that you say? That destiny is prejudice of certain people?"

"Do not make me laugh at your simplicity of mind. By no means is Destiny prejudice of any person! What I am saying is that Destiny does not walk with the slave man. Is Destiny flesh and blood? No. Therefore, I am not speaking of the enslaved flesh and blood of man! Surely you know what I speak of when I say that though one is free on the outside of him, he may very well be enslaved! Though his flesh and blood is free— he may be a slave man! Bound by the rulings of this mortal world! Fear, opinions, the pressure to conform, criticisms, mandatory beliefs and judgments! Destiny cannot walk with one who is bound by the chains of these!"

"I think I understand... I think I see... she is a great, independent, astronomical, universal, cosmic thing!"

"Yes."

"So what about Destiny and the Hall of Doors? Isn't she the one who walks through the hall, closing all the doors but leaving only one open?"

"What is your point?"

"That sounds an awful lot like fate to me!"

"Destiny walks through the Hall of Doors closing all but one; this is not fate in any way or form. First of all, fate doesn't have access to the Hall of Doors! Therefore, she can't even get in there, anyway! There are many doors opened by that which confuses the mind, doors opened by other things, other voices, and others' choices! None of them is what you want! Behind one of those doors abides what you want! Destiny closes all those other doors that are blinding and misleading! Moreover, she doesn't open the one that's for you, *you* open that one, for yourself! She is just not closing it!"

"So, just to make things clear, Destiny and fate... they are not the same?"

"No. Destiny and fate are not the same. They are not even friends and they do not even like each other. One ought to follow and walk with Destiny; disregard fate!"

"How do I disregard fate?"

"By overlooking fear!"

"I want to talk about that boy you love."

"What about him?"

"You are in love with a boy you spent a few days with. You don't even know him."

"And?"

"And so I want to know how! And why! Why do you love him?"

"I love him because when I look at other people, when I look at everyone else... they are all right there, over there! And I am here. I am right here. But when I met him, from the first time I saw him, I looked at him and I saw that he was here with me! He wasn't over there along with everyone else! He was here, right here where I am. Beside me. With me. We were the same!"

"But the two of you... you're not the same! You're two completely different people!"

"We are different; but we are the same."

"How can two be different and the same at once?"

"How do you define difference, simpleton?"

"Well... I think difference is when you are like *this*, he is like *that* and those are two different ways of being!"

"That's not what difference is. Difference is not found in ways of being. Difference is found in *places* of being! We are only different when we are in different places! And when I speak of places, I don't mean the measurements of time and space and physical proximities! You may spend the greatest amount of time with someone and share the same exact space with someone; yet not be in the same place as that same person, at all! And then you meet someone one day, someone whom you have never seen before and you look at the person knowing that you are in the same place!"

"So, these places that you speak of, how do we get there?"

"We do not get there; we are born there! Then, many times we forget where! Destiny brings us back to these places."

"Can you take someone with you to your place?"

"I think yes. Yes, you can take people with you to your place, but only if they were born there and simply forgot where they were born! When they meet you, there is *recognition!* With other people, there is no recognition!"

"What does it feel like... to meet someone who is in the same place as you? Or who was born in the same place as you?"

"You mean someone who is the same as you?"

"Yes. Someone who is the same as you. What does it feel like to meet that person?"

"It feels like nothing you have ever felt before, you want to *stay*. To stay with him. Forever. Because if you stay with him, you will never be alone, you will never be lost again, never!"

"So the boy... you recognized him?"

"Yes, I recognized him. And he recognized me."

"And so you love him?"

"And so I love him."

"How does love happen?"

"There is no telling how love happens! Love is so unbridled and unconquered yet at the same moment, it is so atomic that it is able to penetrate the most basic proofs of existence of the human being and so we have here something greater than all of us! I am not truly surprised by anything as I watch everything while it all unfolds— but Love— Love surprises me!

"Do you believe in love at first sight?"

"Yes, I think that Love comes always at first sight! It does not take that long to recognize someone! You recognize someone at first sight!"

"So where and at what point, do Logic and Reason come into the picture?"

"Logic and reason? But logic and reason are not in the same place as Love! They are not the same! They are different! Love is *here*; logic and reason are *over there*."

"Sort of like the difference between Destiny and fate?"

"Yes, they are not friends! Nevertheless, people want them to work together! Sometimes, even mistake them for one another! Now this— this is the great mistake of mankind!"

"Logic and Reason... who are they friends with?"

"Fear and doubt."

"But I thought fear was fate's friend!"

"Yes, and that's how fate knows logic and reason! Through fear! This is also how fate counteracts Destiny! If you are to obey logic and reason, you will not find Destiny!"

"And what about Love— again— if your love is unbound, unbridled and the twin of Destiny, what about what others think? When does the weight of what others think step into the scenario of your love?"

"What others think bears no weight. Because Love is so dense, alas, the weight of what anybody else thinks becomes useless! There is no gravity! No value! No virtue! The density of Love leaves all gravity powerless! There is no relevance to the question *what do others think*."

"So you're saying... Love is blind?"

"I never think that *blind* is a worthy thing to be and I surely think that of all things, Love is *not* blind! It is just that Love is greater than all of that!"

"It is a recognition?"

"Yes. It is a recognition."

"So Love is never blinded?"

"No. Love sees. And that is why it is in turn seen at first sight!"

"In that way, it is something like a reflection!"

"Well, in a way, recognition *is* a reflection! As you recognize your own reflection, so will you recognize the reflections of those things that are *the same*, that are in the same place as you."

"What about those who love not at first sight? Do you call their love a fake love?"

"What is not fake to a man, is not fake for him. And who am I to call the truth of someone else a falsity, a fake thing?"

"Tell me now, how do God and faith imply each other?"

"God is He whom we cannot see. Faith is that which we need in order to see God."

"See God? Is it even possible to see God?"

"Yes, I see God! With Faith, I see God!"

"See God? How do you see Him?"

"I see God when I look at myself, because I see Him with me! Human souls are from God and without the Spirit of God no one spirit exists! My soul comes from that Absolute Might, that Spark in the darkness of the universe; I am *of* Him! When I look at myself, I see God *with* me. We see the Kingdom of God by the journey of our spirit. Lo and behold— the Kingdom of God is within! As we journey within, we see God more and more! It is a natural occurrence. It is not to be worked for nor strived for."

"Are you actually saying that the union with God, and the quest to see Him, is not a laborious journey? It is not something earned, something that one struggles for, a bondage that man must devote himself to in gaining the final prize?"

"The union of spirit with God is freedom! The only real way we are freed is by finding the door from which we came from! Outside that door is all that we have become as a result of this world! The journey back into ourselves is the journey towards God, because we all have come from God! In God is our freedom! We give ourselves to no bondage in our journeys; we give ourselves to *Freedom!*"

"And this is why you do not believe in having a religion?"

"This is why I believe that no man nor group of people secured by a religion can show his fellow man the way. Because man always adds, subtracts and demands. This is the lack of wholeness, the absence of entirety and the threat of bondage!"

"And the greatest bondage is fear?"

"The greatest bondage is fear."

"Tell me about the spark which you spoke of earlier, the spark in the darkness from which you say you came."

"What about it?"

"How can a single spark in the darkness of a vast universe produce such living things as the human souls?"

"And the Angelic Soul! And other forms of Divine Souls!"

"There are other forms of souls?"

"Most certainly so! And why are you surprised that life can come from darkness? Why, do you think that the light and the darkness are entirely separated and the one did not come from the other and the one is not caused by the absence of the other?"

...

"Even The Almighty is a Spark in the vast darkness! And from this darkness, all life has come forth! Even *you*!"

"Even me?"

"Even you!"

"From something so small?"

"If something is the only thing of it's nature, does that make it small, or does that make it powerful? In an unending, expanding universe filled with darkness and there is a single Spark, does that make it small, or does that make it All-Powerful?"

"All-Powerful?"

"Yes, that is right."

"And so from the single Spark there comes forth all manner of Divine Life and life of all other nature?"

"Where else would it come from?"

"Does anything come forth from the darkness itself?"

"Perhaps. But it is of a less powerful nature and as the darkness conceived the light, so the children of darkness are brought forth as a propitiation for all light."

"So at the end of a great battle, there really is no war?"

"You could say that."

"So, Destiny... how can I *have* her? How can I have her with me? Is there anything that I can do so that I may walk with her, as well? There is nothing I want more than this!"

"Destiny walks with those who know what they want. Many do not truly know what it is that they want, but only know what it is that others want for them. This is a form of bondage. Destiny— she walks hand-in-hand with those who know what they want. You may not know why you want what you want, and it may not even be what you end up getting! You may receive something far better than what you initially wanted. But right here, right now, you have to want something. Something that is *yours!*"

"The right thing?"

"It is not about the right or the wrong of things. It is about what is *yours.*"

"But when we search for Love, we look always for *the right one*; how does this which you say, fit into that which we do?"

"If it is 'the right one' whom you search for, you will never find Love! Love is recognition. So what do you do when the one whom you recognize, doesn't match the 'right' one you have described on your wish lists and in your notebooks? Love is not found in searching for what is 'right;' Love is found in searching for what is *yours*. Love reveals itself to the heart which has gone out in the pursuit to find what is it's *own*. What it wants, what it yearns for, what it so longs for! To identify and to find it! Love does not choose to reveal itself to the heart that has gone out in the pursuit of something 'right.' Because your idea of 'right for you' may not be what awaits you! Love leads you to what awaits you! Destiny leads you to what is yours."

"It sounds to me... it sounds to me like Love and Destiny come to the same person! Are you saying that Love is destined?"

"I am saying that Love and Destiny walk with the same person. It is wise not to label love as destined or as anything, really, because Love is too all-encompassing to be labeled as anything! Nevertheless, in Love is found Destiny, and in Destiny is found Love."

"What about second chances?"

"What about them?"

"What if you get one?

"A second chance?"

"Yes, what if you get a second chance?"

"You take it!"

"But how many chances does one really have in life?"

"I cannot say how many chances one really has in life. Nevertheless, I am sure that life is full of them! Life is made up of chances!"

"But then there is what we call fear, and fear many times gets into the way of one's chances. So, would you say that to find the absence of fear is to find the answers we all look for along our paths of life? Since chances are scattered and fill the potholes all along our paths in life?"

"Yes."

"But what exists in the absence of fear?"

"Happiness!"

"How do I find the absence of fear?"

"The heart who searches for that which is not material, will find the absence of fear."

"Not material?"

freedom from material things realm brings a return to self

"The material is only that— material. Destiny is immaterial, Love is immaterial, trust is immaterial. Fear and the absence of fear— they are both immaterial! Happiness is immaterial! Chances... chances are immaterial and life itself is immaterial! You received fear immaterially and you will find that the absence of it is also immaterial. Freedom is not found in the material; freedom is found in the release from the material! Material bondages are created by the material realm; by the realm consisting of the fragments of what other people think you are and what they think you ought to be like! The things you are made to believe in, in order to control the outcome of your life, and so on and so forth. The fragments that are the parts of the lower realm are developed by the societies of mankind and to escape the enchantment of these fragments is to find Freedom. Therefore, you will find Freedom and the absence of fear together: hand-in-hand."

"Where is true freedom found?"

"True Freedom is found along the path one walks when walking towards God."

"God? But isn't God the One who distinguishes man according to his works? Isn't He who separates the sheep from the goats? Man must run away from God, if he ever is to be free! And especially if he likes goats!"

"God is He whom we all have come from! The Spark in the never-ending darkness! From and in Him all exist! And apart from Him— we will fail to exist in our true form! We enter into the world and our form is instantly altered. Then these alterations are enhanced by the material bondages I have just spoken to you about. Freedom exists and consists of the return to our true form! Our true nature! A return to ourselves is a return to where we have come from! We have come from One God who has said that His Kingdom can be found *within us*! The path towards God is the path towards Freedom. God exists in the absence of fear, we come from the absence of fear! Find yourself and you will lose fear!"

"I want to ask you— about the things that you want— should you still want something even if it looks like you will never have it anyway?"

"Is the something yours?"

"Yes, I think so. Because in my heart I feel it is!"

"Then you should still want it! Because what is yours is yours; even if you do not have it; it's yours! It is in the heart where all is had and all is truly owned! It is also only in the heart where all that is truly lost, is lost! You only really lose something, someone— if you have lost them from your heart!"

"This reminds me of faith. To own what I do not yet have. Is this what faith is like?"

"Maybe."

"Maybe?"

"Maybe, but I don't think it is very important what things are called; I think it is more important what things *are*. There may be many wonderful things out there that we do not know the names of, we don't know what to call them; but there they are! And it does not make them any less there!"

"Do you think humans like to give a name to everything? That people like to know what everything is called?"

"Yes, they do. Also, people like explanations! But some things do not need names and meanings! Some things are just what they are!"

"They often ask what your smile means..."

"People ask what my smile means, but it doesn't mean anything, really. Or maybe it means everything! I'm not really sure, not everything has to mean something! Nevertheless, some things can sometimes mean everything! I think that my smile is just my smile, and then anything else that it wants to be!"

"Can a smile have a will, that you may say *it wants to be?*"

"Who knows? Who knows if every single member of my body has its own will and if this final masterpiece I call my body is but a coming together, an agreement of, a vision, a picture that has become! What if I in my totality, am an agreement of many different parts, many different things? Look, my nose does one thing while my tongue does another thing! My eyes are used for *seeing* the world around me while my ears are used for *hearing* the world around me! Yet, all of these parts agree to make my life a beautiful experience for me! It is all *for me!* I am a coming together of many different things that agree upon one thing: to give me what is beautiful on my journey in this world! Therefore... who knows if my smile has it's own will to be what it wants to be?"

"But sometimes a mind can tell all the members of one's body that nothing at all is beautiful... "

"Yes, and the members of the body begin to fall out of agreement, fall out of unison, fall out of harmony... "

"Is that what sickness is? Disease? Is that what it is, is that how it happens?"

"Perhaps."

"Perhaps?"

"What do you think?"

"I think so."

"I think so, too."

"Do you know that they often question where you come from? They say you are unreal because you exist in fairytales!"

"I am not unreal! And I am not the thing of fairytales! For so long, I have existed in this grey area and in all of this! Everything around me has always been grey! No one can say that I never learned anything the hard way! All the colors I draw— I created these colours, myself! The red, the blue, the green, yellow, violet, aquamarine, pink, purple, lilac— I put those there! I coloured them in! There was no storybook which I arrived into, for me to exist in! I exist first, and *then* I create! No one can say I never learned anything the hard way! No one can say that. Producing colours from grey is not something learned the easy way!"

"They sometimes— some of them— they sometimes wonder why you push people away..."

"I don't think I ever push people away. In fact, I feel like I call them in, even more than I should! But then, perhaps then, when they get too close... maybe then I push them away."

"But why?"

"I am not sure, really... I think it is because it's easier that way."

"Easier?"

"I don't move and tremble, feel and leap, at the same frequency as most people. Their thoughts and emotions eventually become too loud for me to handle. It comes to a point where I feel as though I am standing in front of the loudspeakers at a concert!"

"If their frequencies are different, they become too 'loud' to be around?"

"Some flesh and blood vibrates at a totally different frequency from my own. Unfortunately, that is most people, for me. That is why it has been the most crucial aspect of my life to find others like me, or specifically, one other like me or more powerful than me. So I can feel safe at long last! So I can feel safe, can belong, and can fulfill!"

"But you can't keep on doing this, if you do, then how will you know who you want to stay with? Or who you want to stay with you?"

"I don't run away from people; I think that the only one I run away from is myself. It is frightening to feel so different. Hence, I do not make things hard for me, or for anyone! Things are simply what they are, as they are! But don't overlook the fact that this is all like a fine porcelain which needs to be handled and thought of with much care! For all at the same time, one must be capable of basking in the glorious light of all that is simple and all that is light! Because in the simple and through the light, many great things are received! And this feeling that I feel right now as I say this to you— this right here— is all much greater than many words and many explanations! This state of being that I feel right in this moment. I feel that I will meet someone one day, and I will never push him away. And the reason for that will be simple! The reason for that will be that I simply will not want him to *ever* go away! Therefore, I will *never* push him! Our skin will vibrate as one flesh! And perhaps at the end of the day, all the pushing I have done, is only because they weren't him! Because none of them were him!"

"What is the most difficult thing about hearing the thoughts and sensing the feelings of those who don't share in your own frequency?"

"The most difficult thing is watching them enact something entirely different. It is confusing, terrifying! It is terrifying to watch someone think something, feel something; but then act out on an entirely different basis from what the initial feeling or thought was!"

"What is *being?* What does it mean to simply *be?*"

"To be is to flow and to grow, to be is like a body of water which flows and grows: always flowing, always growing—this is *to be*. We must know *where* to flow and know *how* to grow."

"What does one need to flow and to grow?"

"To be free! You need to be free!"

"If living is being... then the most important thing to find... is it Freedom?"

"With no Freedom there is no God, there is no Love, there is no Destiny, there is no growth, no flow, no vision, no Truth, no being! In Freedom, there is everything!"

"How can everything be found in one thing? Tell me more, I want to know and feel and see, I want to understand!"

"Freedom is a place, an area. It is a higher place. There are some other people that are here, and things that are here which are unseen. But you first have to set yourself free and believe in what you cannot see, believe that there is something more out there. In freedom can be found many devotions: a devotion to love, a desire to believe, a willingness to be happy, a perseverance to have peace. All these unseen things breathe and grow in the unseen soul. A free person is not an uncommitted person, but in a free person you will find a deep devotion, and a desire to be devoted to even more."

"If Freedom is a place, an area... that sounds a lot like Love! Love is a place, too! Love is to recognize, and who you recognize is who is from the same place or in the same place, as you! Yes, Love sounds a lot like Freedom to me now! Very different in fact, from what I have always thought Love to be! And Freedom to be!"

"Freedom is not the absence of commitment, and to be committed to something or to someone does not mean the loss of Freedom. But Freedom exists in the realm of the unbound and to be free is to be committed to that which is a part of the unbound realm. Whatever sets your soul to flight is Freedom. If someone sets your soul to flight, to stay with that person is not to lose Freedom but to stay with that person is to retain Freedom. Together you have what is unbound. Whatever will swell your spirit and give you wings, is Freedom, and it is a fault if you let go of that for the very reason that you are afraid of losing your Freedom and in doing so you have in fact let go of what will keep you unbound."

"Give me a picture of Freedom, let me see this thing that I may look at it's colours and observe how it moves!"

"There are gigantic trees that have grown tall into the winds and the clouds over the thousands of years of their lives, their tops are rustled and tossed by the mists of the atmosphere! Then there are the short trees that do not live for long; they are young with no deep roots and only a few annual rings to tell their stories. The tall, ancient trees sway in the realm of Freedom while the short young trees cannot even raise their branches into that direction of the sky! Now, you are the bird who needs a tree to live in, if you choose to live in the tree that thrives in the realm of Freedom, that does not mean you are not committed to that tree; you are still committed to your tree, but together you and your tree live in Freedom! Freedom is not the absence of commitment. If you are the bird who chooses to fly around amongst the short trees and live in them, that is because your wings are too short to make it any higher and your vision too near to see any further into the clouds! And if you move from one short tree to the next short tree, that does not mean you are free; you are still down there below, Freedom is still nowhere near you!"

"This all means that the multitude of people in the world who think they have found Freedom; don't actually have it! Now I know the answer to why they are so unhappy, why people cannot find happiness! For in Freedom is found happiness! Without Freedom, how can happiness come?"

"Mankind is often arrogant to see itself as possessing things which in fact it has no understanding of. They say each one's perception is a truth.... perhaps perception is a form of truth; in that your perception has the power to alter the forms of the things in your life by changing the way you see them; nevertheless, being a *form* of a truth, is not necessarily *the* Truth, itself!"

"A form of the truth is different from the Truth itself?"

"When from the Spark in the darkness all life forms came into existence, each existence burst forth and bore it's own form of that Almighty Truth. Let's say there was a word that was given life and that word carried on through the centuries; yet that same word changed in form and colour due to time and the persuasion of circumstance, space and material matter— that word would be a *form of the truth*, without being the *Truth Itself!*"

"Is it possible for one to be happy without possessing any internal devotion to any sacred cause such as Serenity, Peace, Love? In other words, is it possible for happiness to exist in the heart of one who has not known true Freedom?"

"A form of happiness, yes, but not Happiness itself."

"But is it not that we should be able to find happiness in the smallest and simplest of things?"

"It is only the free one who finds Happiness in the simplest and in the smallest of things! For in Freedom is harboured Innocence! And it is Innocence that brings Happiness into even the smallest of forms! Innocence has very tiny hands!"

"Innocence has very tiny hands?"

"That reach into the smallest of places!"

"Is not innocence feeble and weak?"

"Not at all! Innocence is power; Innocence is the breath of the gods and the demi-gods! Did you think for one moment that Innocence belongs to the humans? Innocence is the breath of Angels and in Innocence there is true power. There is nothing feeble, nothing weak, about it! For with such small hands it is able to bring itself even into the smallest of things and plant Happiness there in them! This is an act of true power!"

"So Innocence is an attribute of the gods?"

"It is the life force of the gods."

"I always thought that Innocence belonged to the weakest, youngest of us!"

"When people are born, they are born into this world closer to the Initial Spark. As they grow, they grow further away from The Spark. Innocence as a child is not necessarily the companion of the child's helplessness and smallness."

"Tell me about your dreams at night."

"Which ones?"

"The ones that were never just dreams."

"There are dreams in particular, which showed me the path I was to take. I have had many, many dreams and many, many paths; but some in particular— I remember in these certain dreams I am always wearing a long, white dress!"

"As you are now?"

"Yes, as I am now."

"And what were you doing while wearing this dress?"

"In one dream, I was driving a pickup truck and the back was loaded with people! I drove up a steep hill, through all the trees, fast and with much fervor I drove up and up and up! In my soul I knew where I was going and why I was driving the people there; but in my mind I had no idea where I was headed and I had no directions, no map to get there! I just went, I went and I went! I wanted to get the people to the destination as fast as I could! When we reached the top of the mountain, there was a stone wall with a window, I looked through the window and down below I saw a shoreline! Somehow, I remembered where the door to that shore was, and called out to the people to follow me! I told them to come quick, and I ran along the wall that led towards the shoreline down below! Down at the opposite end, at the foot of the mountain, I beheld the entrance of stone that led to the vanilla shoreline! I stood by the door and told the people to go in! One by one, they stepped inside, they walked forward onto the shore and I watched as each one went and walked on, taken into the arms of the air of this place, never to return again! In my heart, as I watched them, my soul glowed with good cheer and contentment!"

"Did you understand what the dream meant?"

"Upon awaking from my dream, I did not understand what it meant and in fact, I was afraid! I thought it meant that I was to be left behind as others went along into the Promised Land! But now I understand my dream, I understand what it meant! I was to lead people to the places unseen because I know where these unseen places are! It is not that I was to be left behind; it is just that I had come from those places, and those places— like that unseen shoreline which enveloped and took the people in— were places of my origin, the place of my birth! I am one with the elements, so naturally I know where the windows and the walls and the entrances are!"

"You speak as though you have had many dreams of this nature!"

"I have. And I had all these dreams far long ago, far before I began to colour things with my songs! Long before I began to colour the winds with my words and change the people! Therefore, my dreams have told me of my Destiny."

"Or do you think Destiny spoke to you through your dreams?"

"Maybe I myself am Destiny, have you thought of that one?"

"No, not yet. But now that you mention it, maybe... but tell me about your other dreams now!"

"There was another dream wherein I was leading many people through an underground tunnel! It was a subway station and I led them over the train tracks, directly heading towards the other side, into the brick wall! Just like in my other dream, I knew not in my mind where I was leading them to; but in my heart I was certain that I knew the way and that they should follow!"

"What happened when you reached the other side of the tracks? When you reached the brick wall?"

"I pushed at the wall with my hand, and opened it!"

"A door appeared?"

"Yes, I pushed open the brick wall as if there was a door there! Then I led the people beyond, into freedom! I led them to the other side of the door where there was an open field and sunlight!"

"And in your mind, you had no idea what lay beyond those subway walls or that you could even push the wall open for the people?"

"I had no idea in my mind; but in my heart I was certain that I knew the way!"

"Is that how you feel when you write to the people?"

"Yes."

"And you believe in this?"

"I believe in this, because I have seen it with mine own eyes!"

"Where? And how? Tell me, I want to know!"

"I was once in Florence, in Italy. There was a man who asked to read the things that I write and so I met him in a restaurant, I handed him my notebook and I watched as he opened it and began to read what I had written in it. I watched the layers of his countenance peel away and fall down! I watched the glowing light of the First Spark penetrate the remaining skins of his outer existence and I found his innocence as well as his safe place where he was serene and illuminated! I saw this all in a matter of a few seconds! After those few seconds his friends called him, distracted him, and he gave me my notebook back."

"You saw him enter onto that shoreline!"

"Yes."

"In everything you touch, there is life!"

"Yes. There is life in all that I touch."

"Tell me... what is beauty?"

"Beauty is the most lofty of all things, after Destiny."

"But it is not more lofty than Destiny?"

"Nay, because it is possible to have Beauty, but without Destiny; that beauty can go nowhere."

"Go nowhere?"

"What is someone with Beauty who is without Destiny? Why, a sitting swan in a cage! With no admirers, with no horizon to meet! No moonlight to bask in, no stream to follow!"

"And Destiny without beauty?"

"There are many of those who are put into lofty places, that possess far less beauty than others who have not been found by Destiny!"

"So after Destiny, Beauty comes most important? But isn't this a shallow way of thinking?"

"If this is a shallow way of thinking, then shall we allow the world to become a thing unsightly to look upon? Shall we allow ourselves to become things ugly to look upon? If this is a shallow way of thinking, then are we to simply allow decay, is that it?"

"But there are those who see nothing *but* Beauty, and look at what kinds of people they are!"

"Oh, it is not Beauty that they see! And it is not Beauty that is being shown to them, either! It is what they have been told Beauty is; it is a program, a presentation! But True Beauty, Pure Beauty, has no need of verification, no need of admonition. True Beauty is a crown in herself, and a crown that she wears upon herself! In and of herself! There need be no crowns made by any other hands, for her!"

"So the shallow people... what they see is not even Beauty at all?"

"When they see Beauty, they will know. They will wonder, they will question, they will ask, they at first will not understand... then they will begin to understand, begin to see, begin to identify, begin to acknowledge, begin to know! And then what they once thought was Beauty, will begin to fade in their eyes, will fall from their eyes like a blindfold, and they will be awakened!"

"That is how powerful Beauty is? It has the power to grant Freedom and vision?"

"Indeed."

"What is grace?"

"Grace is the stuff of Beauty. She is the ability to give, as well as to receive and be thankful— Serenity— the disposition of being able to allow things to flow freely into your fingers and out of your fingers like water. Class. Think of a mermaid who allows the ocean waves to come in and roll out! There is no attempt to control."

"Grace is also a stupendous, powerful thing!"

"Yes, indeed!"

"And what about perfection? I have heard much about perfection, but have not seen it yet! Or have I? Maybe I have seen it, and not known it? What is it?"

"The only people who can see perfection, are those who are looking down from up above, those who see the whole picture in it's entirety. Perfection is like a seashell: If you look at it too closely, all you will see is a strange difficulty and confusion; but if you are the one to hold that same sea shell in your hand, you will see the beauty of the entire design in it's wholeness! In other words, if you are down there in that shell, nothing will look perfect to you; but unbeknownst to you, you are dwelling within a perfect design, without seeing its perfection! The one holding the shell, on the other hand, can see the wholeness of that shell, along with you inside of it!"

"How many of there are you who can hold the shell in their hand?"

"God holds the big shell with all of us inside of its pattern! And, alas, some of us hold smaller shells in our hands, too! So far, I have only known myself, and none other than I. I wish to meet others, but simply haven't yet. The shell I hold is a small one, though! And oftentimes, even I cannot see the whole pattern! Fear and doubt take my vision of the pattern away all too often."

"What must one do to hold a shell in their hand and look at it from a distance?"

"I cannot answer that question, there is nothing I have practiced in order to hold a shell in my hand this way. Perhaps it is simply given and simply received, perchance it is given to those who have no desire to control anything— those who simply receive. Let me tell you a story of a Princess of a great Kingdom! She faced a daily internal dilemma: was she powerful because she could control everything; or was she powerful because she could simply receive everything? The two choices stood in front of her, every day, and often she chose control which brought her only distress; until the day that she accepted that things were simpler than that!"

"Things were simpler than that? How so?"

"It was difficult for her to simply receive such great things and such cosmically-proportioned gifts and because of this to realize her importance! It was easier for her to think that because she could wield her sceptre and control everything, she was powerful because of that! Sometimes the acceptance of the simpler is the more difficult thing to do. But for some, power lies in the act of simply knowing that many things are *given* to you, and you only have to *receive* them!"

"And so it is like the shell in your hand?"

"Yes, it is like the shell in my hand."

"Why didn't God place the shell into everyone's hand?"

"If God did that, then who would comprise the design? If all were to step out of the shell, who would be inside the shell?"

"Is it a lesser state of being— not to be able to hold the shell?"

"It is a different state of being, we are different. Just as the body and the soul are different— neither is lesser! If you kill the body, you remove the destiny of the soul from this earth! And if you neglect the soul, you remove the meaning for being on this earth!"

"And if there were no earth?"

"What do you mean by that?"

"The common denominator of both body and soul is the earth– now– what if the earth did not exist? Would not holding the shell be a lesser state of existence?"

"In all designs, none is equal. To wish for equality is to wish for imperfection. All parts of the whole create a perfect design. People are *part of the perfect.*"

"Are some people perfect?"

"You mean in and of themselves?"

"Yes, in and of themselves."

"There are people who are a gathering of many difficult and confusing things, which glue together as a design that when looked upon as a shell in the hand— is indeed perfect. But even the many who do not glue together into something perfect; are given purpose in the scheme of the whole."

"So even in the absence of perfection, there still lies purpose?"

"Precisely."

"What things are found in the final, perfect design?"

"Therein are found Serenity, harmony, symphony."

"It sounds like Serenity plays a role in two very important things! Both Beauty and Perfection!"

"Serenity is like the mist that rises above an ocean in the early mornings. Even if the water underneath is tossed and turned by inner turbulence; that all remains unseen; while the thick, white mists hover above— like *merachefet*."

"And that is why Serenity plays a role in such important things! Because it is the likeness of *merachefet*!"

"Exactly. It is the likeness of power. But it is more than just a likeness! It is the actual face of merachefet! It is how you identify merachefet!"

"And symphony and harmony?"

"They are what come along with Serenity. If there is Serenity, there is symphony and harmony."

"Can there be symphony and harmony without Serenity?"

"There are different symphonies and different harmonies; they can come from a variety of sources that are not serene. There is certain chaos, which can produce a symphony! A certain loss, which can produce a harmony! But where there be Serenity, there is always symphony and harmony which follow!"

"What about humility? They say humility is good, but just how good is humility, just how beneficial is it?"

"Humility is like a transparent curtain made of effervescent strings of gold that sway in the winds like silk! This curtain falls over one's skin like a wedding veil, wedding one to all things Divine! There is no man or woman who is capable of receiving anything Divine without living in the skin of Humility, without his or her skin being bathed in the silken, golden waters of Humility! There is nothing Divine that can penetrate without the loss of ego! And the loss of ego results in Humility! Humility is both Beautiful and Divine!"

"Ego is like an outer crust on a man or woman?"

"It's worse than an outer crust, because it takes root! It is not developed from the outside in; but it is developed from the inside out! Like a weed that chokes the true rose— the ego chokes the true soul!"

"And Humility both bathes the soul and veils the skin?"

"Indeed."

"And the result would be something beautiful, am I right?"

"Beautiful, indeed!"

"Without Humility, there can be no Beauty?"

"The ego, like an inborn, adaptable parasite that attaches itself and merges itself with every cell of the human body, mutating it into a form of the parasite itself— is the perfect form of ugly! With ego, there is no Beauty!"

"But isn't the ego one's own self?"

"Ego is the self of itself; not really the self of the soul. It is a reflection of itself alone; not a reflection of the entire (what there is and was and is to come!) No person can be all that he/she can be, while harboring the ego!"

"And yet the ego is the one telling the person that he or she is all that he or she can be!"

"Exactly. A blind contentment! A stupid contentment, which leads to nothing but stagnancy and a pitiful stupor! A satisfaction not worthy of its own self."

"That is why it is so difficult to accept that one's power lies in simply receiving! Because it takes Humility to accept that! To accept that you are simply special therefore much is given to you; not that you have more because you can control more— that calls for Humility!"

"Yes, you understand well. Ego pushes for a need to prove something to one's self and prove something to others. The birthright is forgotten and forsaken in favor of a sceptre! But is it the sceptre that wields the power? Or is it the simple birthright?"

"It is the birthright, indeed. Without the birthright, the sceptre is nothing, after all!"

"You have understood well."

"Shall we have mercy on those with ego? Do you have mercy on the egotistical?"

"Mercy is something which I have been recently learning about and coming to truly understand. When I possessed less power, I did not have the ability to feel mercy; it is only with an increase in power that I am able to adopt the qualities of having mercy. Mercy, I have come to know, is not a weakness; rather, it is a culmination of strength! I am able to look upon the egotistical person through eyes of mercy because I am fully aware that I can easily destroy him simply by a single wish, a single trickle of desire in my heart to see his downfall. As you can see, along with great power comes great awareness of what the power can do as well as the understanding enough to see that because someone is so easily crushed, because it is such an easy task to accomplish, there is no valor in doing it!"

"So what was once a trait to be acquired, becomes something of less courage to do?"

"Yes. It was difficult for me to feel any mercy at all when I was less aware of the power that was mine. Now as I see the power that I have, I am capable of having mercy. If power is given to a wicked soul— he will lose all ability to be merciful. When power is given to a Divine soul— that soul will acquire mercy."

"What if the person deserves to be crushed?"

"If that is what he deserves, then after coming into contact
with the one who has the power to do that, the simple
contact with that power alone is already sufficient to bring
him to his ruin. A power is not necessarily a conscious act;
but in its purest form, it is a presence. Let me tell you of a
dream that I had— in my dream I saw a poisonous snake
and in much gentleness I walked up to this snake, picked it
up softly and at the mere touch of my skin the serpent
began to spasm and to convulse! It then began to vomit out
it's own innards and there died in my hand by means of
vomiting it's own internal organs, then paralysis by which it
became stupefied like a stick! It became nothing but a
lifeless, inert, stupefied serpent! Moreover, this all
happened while I held it softly in my hands, exerting no
effort whatsoever! I felt my own power, it was a presence, it
was my own presence and it thrived in my own skin! There
was no reason for me to feel anger or vengeance towards
the snake! There was no need for me to exert any amount
of effort! What happened to the snake had nothing to do
with my emotions and feelings; it simply had to do with
the touch of my skin!"

"So there is no struggle to overcome one's enemies, no
struggle to punish the wicked?"

"Does a candlelight struggle to give light in a dark room?"

"No, it is just there."

"Exactly— it is just there."

XLII

"In that case, mercy is not actually an attribute of the light, but also an attribute of the darkness?"

"When a candle is lit in a dark room, can we say that the attributes of the flame belong to the candle alone, or should we say that to have light within darkness, is also an attribute of darkness?"

"Just as there are stars in the night skies?"

"Yes."

"The twinkling of the stars is not only an attribute of the bodies of mass themselves; but has become an attribute of the night both in our imagination and in our beliefs!"

"Yes, you understand well."

"So mercy is both dark and light, as the stars are to the night heavens and the flame is to a dark room?"

"Indeed."

"It must be so, I guess, since the merciful one is not necessarily a beacon of light, but could very well be the presence of a magnanimous, terrible power!"

"Oh but power is always magnanimous and terrible. Terrible in that it can freeze your skin without a change in temperature! It can cause you to tremble without the slightest threat. There are results simply because of the presence."

"And this is how God is powerful?"

"Most likely, yes. Because God hovers, God is in merachefet and through merachefet even the fallen sparks are brought to life again."

"Tell me about how you stand in the doorway in the wee hours of the morning! Long before the sun arises, who is it whom you await?"

"Oh— you know about that? Yes, I stand in the door with it half open, as if he whom I wait for will enter any moment! For so long, my heart has longed, yearned— I wait eagerly and for what or for whom, I am not sure! I feel that if I stand there and if I wait there, eagerly with my eyes scanning the distant darkness, I will be able to catch him when he arrives! It is as if I know for certain that right now is the time, that right here is the place where he will be arriving and yet I do not truly know for whom or for what I stand and wait!"

"What does that feel like?"

"It feels exactly like what it looks like. It feels like standing in a half-open door alone, looking and searching into the darkness beyond, waiting and waiting for someone or something to arrive! It feels just how it looks! Desolate— but full of anticipation!"

"I wonder if your thoughts turn to other things in the morning. For you, the darkness is filled with eager anticipations. And so, I wonder what your mornings are like? To where do your thoughts turn? Or to whom do your thoughts turn?"

"My thoughts turn to the ways of God in the morning! I remember His ways of old, and I can see Him now in the mornings, for He is steadfast like the sunrise! His steadfastness is still and everlasting throughout all generations... His tenderness and love like the morning dew. The paths He has laid out for me are ones of peace! Freedom is the wind that picks up His wings! He is always with me, and He is always the same!"

"But that sounds... it sounds very much like a love story!"

"It has always been a love story! It has always been just that!"

"What do you think, is the most important thing about being in love with someone?"

"I think there is no need to advertise the relationship. The love should advertise the relationship; not the relationship which should advertise the love. Love is stronger and goes far beyond any agreements and all descriptions! It is not the marriage contract that holds any eternal importance; it is only the love that does! A ring is a beautiful symbol but it is only that, a symbol! Love is unconquered by any matter having to do with space and with distance or with nearness and time! Similarly, I do not need to classify myself as a Christian or a Gentile or a Muslim or a Jew. I have a love story with God! This is not my religion; I am on a journey! A journey which is called life! And on this journey, I have a love story with God; that is not a religion! That is an odyssey!"

"What are the things that you believe in? I mean those certain things that you really, really believe in?"

"I don't believe in everything that I can see. Rather, I believe in everything I can't see that I know!"

"But what is there that cannot be seen, that you believe in? And if I am to believe in things I cannot see, what would I be believing in?"

"I do not believe in anything that I don't know. There are many things that I can see but I do not *know*. What I do know, is that I know Love, I know Destiny, Freedom, I know fear, mercy, Serenity, Beauty... I know many things that can't be seen in material form! If you only believe in what you can see, you cannot know the things that I know! You cannot believe in your instincts, not even in your own doubts! For all of these are unseen! You cannot even believe in yourself, because look at you! You are a soul!"

"I thought you said that fear is your enemy! But now you include it among those things that you know!"

"Yes, fear is my enemy, and that's why I know it so well! It is essential to know one's enemies! Then one will know how to deal with them!"

"Oh what about God! God is something unseen!"

"Yes, this is true."

"Does this mean that you know God?"

"Yes of course, yes I do!"

"Who is He?"

"I call Him the Alpha and Omega, I call Him Abba. He is the God of all gods, and all gods bow a knee before Him!"

"How do you know God?"

"We all know Him; but we just forget. And I— I have just remembered. It's nothing unique."

"But how can you know things that are unseen?"

"If I remember it, then I know it. I remember things most people have forgotten. When you know something or when you know someone, you remember many things about it or about him/her. Just because you can see something or someone, that doesn't mean you can remember anything, that doesn't mean that you have knowledge of the thing or the person. It doesn't mean that you *know*! I will judge nothing or no one based upon what I can see with my eyes; but I will judge based upon what I know with my heart, regardless of what anybody else says or thinks."

"So when you love someone, is this how you love someone?"

"Yes, I love with my heart."

"And so if you love with your heart, that probably means you want to be loved through the heart, too, am I right?"

"Yes. Love fulfilled is a love which recognizes the other and can find recognition in the other, also."

"I was wondering... what happens when you try to get somewhere but you don't make it to that destination?"

"Why ask this now?"

"I was just thinking— of all the things you know, all the unseen things— I simply thought, what if you are trying to get somewhere and you didn't? Then what happens? Something as simple as that, what does it mean?"

"Like if you're trying to get to the Trevi Fountain?"

"Yes, somewhere like the Trevi Fountain. What if you were trying to get to it but you couldn't find it?"

"What about it?"

"Does that mean something bad? If you tried to get somewhere but you couldn't?"

"No, it doesn't mean something bad. It just means that there is a next time. And having a next time is better than having just one time!"

"Like a second chance?"

"Yes, like a second chance. Two chances are always better than just one!"

"How do people grow?"

"What do you mean?"

"How do people grow and how do they get better?"

"Growth is only possible if there is something to grow into. The only way to become better is by the opening of the eyes and identifying of what is better in front of you. You will only become better if, when you look in front of you, you can see what is better than you are and you can identify that and learn from that. The only way to grow is by looking at the taller trees and seeing how much taller you have to grow, by looking at that and by accepting it. The only way to fly is by looking up into the skies and seeing the heights far above you. You can only fly if you look up and see that you are down here and there is so much more up there that you can know; but you must first see this! If when you open your eyes, you see nothing better than yourself— you will never become any better than you already are! And if when you look at the taller trees, you bring out a chainsaw and attempt to cut those trees down, you will still be as low as you are now and if you do succeed at sawing those trees to the ground; that still will not make you any taller than you already are right now! If, upon looking up into the sky, you see no soaring heights, you will never grow wings and learn how to fly! If you want everything else to always be equal to where you are now, you will always be only where you are now while others around you continue to look up and to fly, soar and grow! Others will become better and better, growing taller and taller, always flying higher and higher! If you have an affiliation with envy, you will not grow, you will not get any better, you will never fly! The removal of envy, the plucking out of envy from its roots, is what is essential to mankind if it is to grow, transform, get any better!"

"Are you happy right now?"

"I am very happy right now, yes!"

"What is Happiness?"

"Happiness is Freedom and Freedom is Happiness."

"Freedom from what?"

"Freedom from the critical, the critical thinking of mankind. The urge to always ask 'why?'"

"To ask why is critical? To ask why of what?"

"To ask why he is happy or why she is happy. He asks himself 'why am I happy?' or 'why should I be happy?' and this is the critical thinking of man and what is critical to him will prevent him from flying and what will prevent him from flying will prevent him from finding Freedom. Moreover, without Freedom, there is no Happiness! We must be free from what we *think* is ourselves and come into what is *truly* ourselves."

"How do you do that? How do you become free from what you think is yourself and come into what is truly yourself?"

"I will not give you a 'how' because a 'how' is not a simple happening. A thing that simply happens does not have a 'how' attached to it. The thing you ask how to do: it is a simple happening— something that simply happens! And this is what I am— I am the one who has ceased to ask 'why?' and there has become no reason for an understanding of the answers of 'why?' and there has become no need to ask 'why?' or 'how?' and I am happy because I am happy. In this I am free, in Freedom I am made happy again, and through this all, I have truly begun to soar!"

"This feels like something powerful."

"It is, Happiness *is* something powerful. To know Happiness is to have power."

"How does Happiness arrive?"

"Happiness wants to be recognized as entirely different and self-sufficient— she will not arrive at the door of one who does not recognize her self-sufficiency. She does not knock on the door of one who says 'I will be happy when I have this' or 'I will be happy when this happens.' Happiness: she does not like to be seen as an accessory to anything, or to anyone else, rather, she wants to be recognized as an entirety and something whole, complete, and sufficient within itself. When you acknowledge her nature— that is when she will step through your door to stay! Open your door to her, and throw the unanswered things out of your window! Happiness will refuse to become an accessory to your still-unanswered longings! Happiness wishes to be in the spotlight! She will not arrive if you are expecting other things before her, other things in order for her to come in! You have to expect her above all else and then she will arrive and step into that beam of light that awaits her. Therefore, to receive Happiness in, there must be strength to look past circumstances and Serenity to feel beyond one's binding outer extremities!"

"Serenity seems to be essential to all good things!"

"Indeed."

"But how can you possibly be ready for Happiness when your circumstances are painful, when all around you everything is blown away or torn down or burning into ashes?"

"It is a very difficult thing, yes, but the key to that is Serenity. The key to many things is Serenity and sure enough to this! The skill lies in the ability to see your inner self. Your inner self is as the eye of a storm: untouched and immovable while the winds reach super speeds hurtling all around! It is very difficult to do this and requires honed skills and strength of steel! I used to depend on God for this; but when He pushed me away, I needed to depend on myself and later I understood why God pushed me away! Because there is a purer form of Serenity and that is one that comes from within yourself! God wants to give, yes, but better than that, He wants you to discover what you already have, what you can do, what He has *already* given! I have found the most effective way to do this is by making the whole world a mirror that you can reflect your inner self upon! In all circumstances, situations, predicaments, hardships, turning points— in the middle of questions and in the midst of answers— perform a spiritual hermetic upon everything! Transform the overlaying material of everything into a mirror clear enough to reflect to you your inner image! The whole world and everything in it should be a mirror that will reflect to you your image, for you to reflect upon! It is in this way that in all things you will be able to have Serenity! By seeing the image of you positioned in Serenity, draped and crowned with Serenity!"

"That is a skill far beyond my own capabilities!"

"They say alchemical magic is in the transformation of any metal into gold; but I say hermetic magic, true magical skill, is the ability to transform any material surrounding your soul into a reflective surface for your own benefit, for the mirroring of your spirit! *This* is a pure alchemy! One that remains obscure to some, one that some did not find!"

"True gold is Serenity."

"Yes."

"When things truly wound a heart— how does the heart recover? And in the first place, if there is a true gold within and a real God without, why do hearts even get wounded, how can it be allowed to happen?"

"You know... even the gods come down here to experience the process of Healing!"

"Gods don't heal in their own realm?"

"Gods lack in nothing, but the experience of Healing creates such an ambrosial aroma, like incense, that even the gods wish to become saturated in such a fragrance!"

"A god would join the masses of humanity, just to experience something that is a result of pain?"

"Healing is not the result of pain, nay, but Healing is the reason for pain! If there were no pain, there would be no chance to heal! If there were no brokenness, there would be no refining of the perfect flame! First, comes brokenness, fear, resulting in the loss of ego; then during the process of healing, the all-perfect flame is ignited! This flame burns an incense (Healing) which produces an aroma so ambrosial, even the gods have longed to smell of such a fragrance."

"By gods you speak of the realm of the angels, am I right?"

"Yes, those formed of the Heavenly realms such as Angels."

"What happens during the process of Healing, how does it become something so beautiful?"

"If you are quickly given to Healing, you will find it is a rapturous uplifting, like the spreading of wings!"

"But don't all angelic creatures have wings? Why seek out Healing to have such an experience?"

"Some pottery that becomes broken is mended with gold, thus becoming even more beautiful in the end, for having been broken! To become even more beautiful— that is the enticement of it all. That is not to say that we should break ourselves or seek out ways to hurt ourselves, definitely not! But if one must experience pain, then one must look forward to the Healing with earnest desire not to look back and not to hurt again; but to fly with the wings of Healing! No desire for pain or loss must ever be produced, nay, but even to heal in earnest *just once in a lifetime*, is to smell of this incense forever!"

"Is there something uniquely beautiful in being human? What is it about the humans, if there is anything, that is uniquely beautiful to them?"

"The beauty of a human lies in his/her ability to be both broken and whole, at the same time! In being able to be not just happy, not just sad; but in having the ability to smile through tears, the ability to love through suffering, the ability to stand when pushed down! It is a small thing and nothing to be arrogant about; but it is a beautiful thing, nonetheless! There are many forms of Beauty, but this is the human's form of it!"

"Does this mean, that in order to be beautiful, one must never be fully whole, fully happy, fully content?"

"Absolutely not. This beauty lies in the *potential* to be both broken and whole at the same time, it is the fabric of the human that contains this potential, which in turn expresses this beauty, it is a certain color dye to the silk! Remember what I said— that to heal in earnest even just once in this lifetime is good enough to smell of the fragrance of Healing! It is never the brokenness that must be sought after; it is the receiving of the gifts that should be accepted!"

"What are memories? How do they happen? Are they simply retentions of things that have happened to you, or are they more than that? Remember that time your future self visited your then present self? How could that have happened, if a memory is indeed only the mind's retention of things that have happened in one's life? You cannot possibly 'remember' yourself from a time that has not even happened yet!"

"Let me tell you something... in all of my 'memories' of my childhood and even my infant years, I am actually standing beside myself and looking at myself! People ask me how I could possibly remember my infancy and I once believed that I simply had a powerful brain— that was until I realized that in all my 'memories' I was actually standing *beside* myself! It is not in first-person! I asked others if their memories unveil in that way and they said not! Their memories always take the form of first-person! Then I compared that to being visited by my future self and in that moment I realized that I have been visiting myself, all throughout my life— my memories aren't actual memories, but they are recollections of the visits that I have made into my past! If I had not been visited by my future self, I would have never realized this!"

"What was it like?"

"To be visited my future self?"

"Yes, what was it like?"

"I was overwhelmed, I paled in comparison to that form of myself! I faded into the distant shadows in the brightness of myself and I felt insignificant, to say the least! She smiled at me with knowing eyes, she was serene, at peace, she was happy! She had everything she ever wanted and she was finally free! But she wasn't a ghost, she wasn't dead! In fact, she was just riding a bus before she visited me! She was wearing the same blue leather jacket that I have right now and it is because of that small detail that I realized she wasn't from a too distant future, because she still owned the same jacket!"

"Did she tell you that everything was going to be okay?"

"She didn't have to, I could feel it emanating from her eyes— the knowing look— she knew exactly the pain I bore, she knew of (and in exact quantities) the crucible that I carried! She *knew*. Because she was there not so long ago! But she also knew that soon it would all be over and far away!"

"Is it all over now? Is it far away now? Do you feel you have crawled out of those shadows and into that brightness already?"

"I still have my jacket... and I am planning to use it soon... maybe I'm almost there? Not quite, but almost!"

"What was the best part about meeting yourself from the future? Was it the new knowledge that everything was going to be okay?"

"It was that look in her eyes and the new knowledge that one day, it would be me who has it! It was the reassuring smile on her face and the knowledge that it would one day be the smile I see in the mirror."

Indulca mei radices.

It is never really the end . . .

The main typeface of the body of this book is set in 12 pt. Centaur, while most other text in this work of literature is also derived from Renaissance origins.

Centaur is a typeface belonging to the *Humanist Family* and was first designed in 1914 by Bruce Rogers for the *Metropolitan Museum of Art*, New York City. The typeface is named after the publication it was first used in: Maurice de Guérin's *The Centaur*, (printed in an edition of 660 copies at the Press of the Wooly Whale) and is based upon several Renaissance models, mainly on roman type by Nicolas Jenson, Venice, 1469.

"For all-time most beautiful face, I nominate Bruce Rogers' Centaur. It's not a general-purpose face at all, like the usual Times or Helvetica (the latter still has a beauty that is underappreciated); but Centaur lives nobly on a page and yet invites its readers to honor both it and its message with their own intelligence and understanding."

— Gary Munch

Printed in Great Britain
by Amazon.co.uk, Ltd.,
Marston Gate.